NATURAL WONDERS
JURASSIC COAST

by Katie Chanez

Ideas for Parents and Teachers

Pogo Books let children practice reading informational text while introducing them to nonfiction features such as headings, labels, sidebars, maps, and diagrams, as well as a table of contents, glossary, and index.

Carefully leveled text with a strong photo match offers early fluent readers the support they need to succeed.

Before Reading

- "Walk" through the book and point out the various nonfiction features. Ask the student what purpose each feature serves.
- Look at the glossary together. Read and discuss the words.

Read the Book

- Have the child read the book independently.
- Invite them to list questions that arise from reading.

After Reading

- Discuss the child's questions. Talk about how they might find answers to those questions.
- Prompt the child to think more. Ask: Did you know about the Jurassic Coast before reading this book? What more would you like to learn about it?

Pogo Books are published by Jump!
5357 Penn Avenue South
Minneapolis, MN 55419
www.jumplibrary.com

Copyright © 2025 Jump! International copyright reserved in all countries. No part of this book may be reproduced in any form without written permission from the publisher.

Library of Congress Cataloging-in-Publication Data

Names: Chanez, Katie, author.
Title: Jurassic Coast / by Katie Chanez.
Description: Minneapolis, MN: Jump!, Inc., [2025]
Series: Natural wonders | Includes index.
Audience: Ages 7-10
Identifiers: LCCN 2024034446 (print)
LCCN 2024034447 (ebook)
ISBN 9798892135436 (hardcover)
ISBN 9798892135443 (paperback)
ISBN 9798892135450 (ebook)
Subjects: LCSH: Anning, Mary, 1799-1847–Juvenile literature.
Fossils–England–Jurassic Coast–Juvenile literature.
Paleontology–England–Jurassic Coast–Juvenile literature.
Geology–England–Jurassic Coast–Juvenile literature.
Jurassic Coast (England)–Juvenile literature.
Classification: LCC QE714.5 .C478 2025 (print)
LCC QE714.5 (ebook)
DDC 560.941–dc23/eng/20240909
LC record available at https://lccn.loc.gov/2024034446
LC ebook record available at https://lccn.loc.gov/2024034447

Editor: Alyssa Sorenson
Designer: Molly Ballanger

Photo Credits: Pajor Pawel/Shutterstock, cover; Robert Harding Video/Shutterstock, 1; Aaron J Seltzer/Shutterstock, 3; Mark Godden/Shutterstock, 4; Anfanisa/Shutterstock, 5; MGodden/iStock, 6-7; serts/iStock, 8; Ianm35/iStock, 9; Mypurgatoryyears/iStock, 10-11; Thomas Faull/iStock, 12-13; Mark Bauer/Loop Images/SuperStock, 14-15; Sarah2/Shutterstock, 16; Finnbarr Webster/Getty, 17; Blaize Pascall/Alamy, 18-19; Fulcanelli/Shutterstock, 20-21; N.M.Bear/Shutterstock, 23.

Printed in the United States of America at Corporate Graphics in North Mankato, Minnesota.

TABLE OF CONTENTS

CHAPTER 1
Rocky Coast 4

CHAPTER 2
How It Formed 8

CHAPTER 3
Finding Fossils 16

QUICK FACTS & TOOLS
At a Glance 22
Glossary 23
Index 24
To Learn More 24

CHAPTER 1
ROCKY COAST

Waves crash along England's southern coast. Tall cliffs tower over the water. This is the Jurassic Coast.

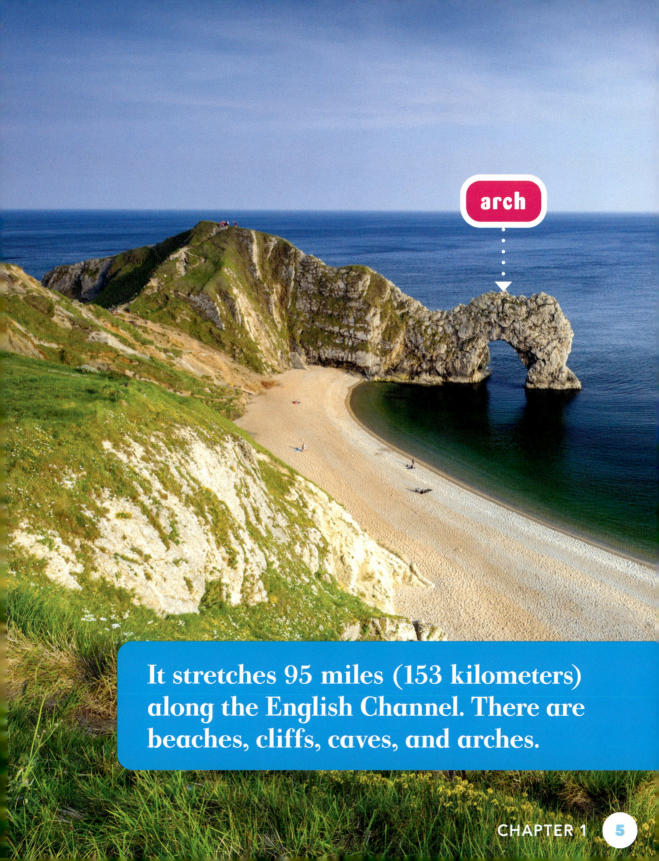

arch

It stretches 95 miles (153 kilometers) along the English Channel. There are beaches, cliffs, caves, and arches.

CHAPTER 1

The rocks here have been forming for more than 185 million years! This place is named after the **Jurassic Period**. Why? **Fossils** from that time period are found here.

DID YOU KNOW?

The Jurassic Period took place 200 to 145 million years ago. Dinosaurs and other **extinct** creatures lived on Earth then.

CHAPTER 1

CHAPTER 2
HOW IT FORMED

The Jurassic Coast is made of **layers** of rock. Scientists study them. The rock tells us what Earth was like in the past. It tells us how the Jurassic Coast formed.

More than 200 million years ago, Earth looked different. The **continents** were connected. What is now England was near the center. It was dry and hot.

Earth 250 million years ago

CHAPTER 2

Layers of sand built up. Sand on top pushed down. **Pressure** hardened the sand beneath. It formed sedimentary rock.

Over time, **tectonic plates** pulled the continents apart. Ocean water covered the area. Mud, sand, and other **sediment** piled up. These also hardened into sedimentary rock.

CHAPTER 2

Over time, the **sea level** rose and fell. Sometimes the area was covered in water. **Algae** in the water sank to the bottom. Over time, the algae hardened into chalk.

WHAT DO YOU THINK?

The Jurassic Coast changed over time. What is one place near you that has changed? How has it changed? What do you think caused those changes?

CHAPTER 2

Erosion created the cliffs, arches, and caves along the coast. Ocean animal fossils were uncovered.

14 CHAPTER 2

TAKE A LOOK!

How does a fossil form? Take a look!

1 A creature dies. Its body breaks down. Hard parts like bones are left behind.

2 Sediment piles on top. It hardens into rock.

3 Water drips through the rock.

4 **Minerals** in water fill the bone. The bone hardens into a fossil.

5 The rock wears away. The fossil is uncovered.

CHAPTER 3
FINDING FOSSILS

People have come here for hundreds of years. Mary Anning was one. Her family found fossils along the coast in the early 1800s.

Mary Anning statue

In 1811, Mary and her brother found a strange fossil. It looked like a monster! They found one of the first *Ichthyosaurus* fossils. This water animal lived about 195 million years ago. Mary was only 12 years old when they found it!

Ichthyosaurus fossil

CHAPTER 3   17

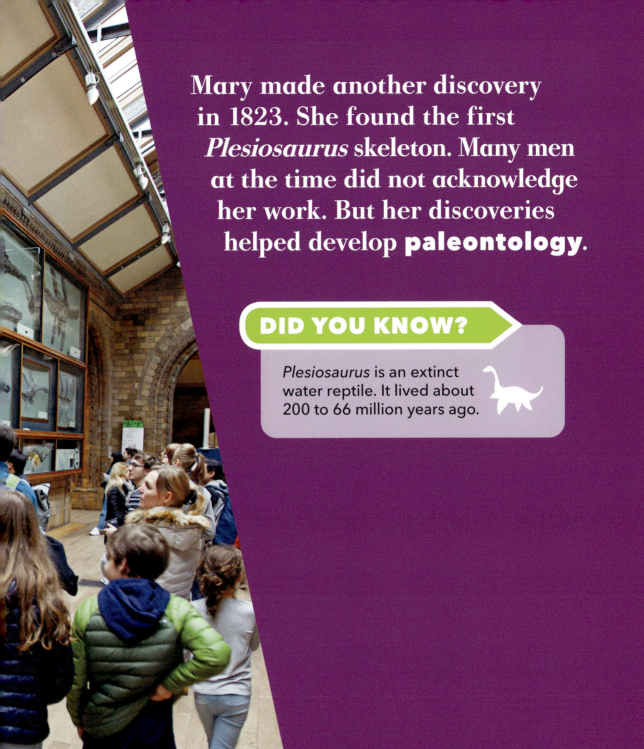

Mary made another discovery in 1823. She found the first *Plesiosaurus* skeleton. Many men at the time did not acknowledge her work. But her discoveries helped develop **paleontology**.

DID YOU KNOW?

Plesiosaurus is an extinct water reptile. It lived about 200 to 66 million years ago.

CHAPTER 3

Millions of people visit the Jurassic Coast every year. They visit the beaches. They hike and boat. They search for fossils! What else might be discovered?

WHAT DO YOU THINK?

Would you like to visit the Jurassic Coast? What would you want to do?

CHAPTER 3

QUICK FACTS & TOOLS

AT A GLANCE

JURASSIC COAST

Location:
southern coast of England

Date Formed:
about 200 million years ago

How It Formed:
layers of sediment hardened into rock and eroded

Number of Yearly Visitors:
about 5 million people

GLOSSARY

algae: Small plants without roots or stems that grow mainly in water.

continents: The seven large landmasses of Earth including Asia, Africa, Europe, North America, South America, Australia, and Antarctica.

erosion: The process of wearing away with water, wind, heat, or ice.

extinct: No longer alive and only known about through fossils or history.

fossils: Bones, shells, or other traces of animals or plants from millions of years ago preserved as rock.

Jurassic Period: A period of time that lasted from 200 million years ago to 145 million years ago.

layers: Parts of something that lie over or under other parts.

minerals: Hard substances found on Earth that do not come from animals or plants.

paleontology: The science that deals with fossils and other ancient life-forms.

pressure: The force produced by pressing on something.

sea level: The average height of Earth's oceans.

sediment: Minerals, mud, gravel, or sand, or a combination of these, that have been carried to a place by water, wind, or glaciers.

tectonic plates: Large, flat sheets of rock that make up Earth's crust.

QUICK FACTS & TOOLS

INDEX

algae 13
Anning, Mary 16, 17, 19
arches 5, 14
chalk 13
cliffs 4, 5, 14
coast 4, 14, 16
continents 9, 10
dinosaurs 7
Earth 7, 8, 9
England 4, 9
English Channel 5
erosion 14
fossils 7, 14, 15, 16, 17, 20
Ichthyosaurus 17
Jurassic Period 7
layers 8, 10
paleontology 19
Plesiosaurus 19
pressure 10
rocks 7, 8, 10, 15
sea level 13
tectonic plates 10

TO LEARN MORE

Finding more information is as easy as 1, 2, 3.

❶ **Go to www.factsurfer.com**
❷ **Enter "JurassicCoast" into the search box.**
❸ **Choose your book to see a list of websites.**

24 QUICK FACTS & TOOLS